HEAD of the CLASS

"I don't have my homework. My dog deleted it."

The Collected *Kappan* Cartoons
for Educators

 Solution Tree | Press

a division of

Solution Tree

The Professional
Association in
Education

 PDK

International

555 North Morton Street
Bloomington, IN 47404
800.733.6786 (toll free) / 812.336.7700
FAX: 812.336.7790

email: info@solution-tree.com
solution-tree.com

Printed in the United States of America

13 12 11 10 09   1 2 3 4 5

FSC
Mixed Sources
Product group from well-managed
forests and other controlled sources

Cert no. SW-COC-002283
www.fsc.org
© 1996 Forest Stewardship Council

Library of Congress Cataloging-in-Publication Data

Head of the class : the collected Kappan cartoons for educators.
    p. cm.
  ISBN 978-1-935249-36-8
  1. Education--Caricatures and cartoons. 2. Learning and scholarship-- Caricatures and cartoons. 3. American wit and humor, Pictorial. I. Phi Delta Kappan.
  NC1428.P53 2009
  741.5'6973--dc22
                          2009028264

President: Douglas Rife
Publisher: Robert D. Clouse
Director of Production: Gretchen Knapp
Managing Editor of Production: Caroline Wise
Project Editor: Kari Gillesse
Proofreader: Elisabeth Abrams
Text Designer: Raven Bongiani
Cover Designer: Amy Shock

Table of Contents

Foreword

In the late 1980s, Avner Ziv, a clinical psychologist teaching at the University of Tel Aviv, conducted a couple of seminal studies concerning humor and teaching and learning. In one case Ziv, who studied under Jean Piaget and earned his PhD at the Sorbonne in Paris, constructed an experiment with students in a fourteen-week class on statistics. The students were randomly chosen to take the same class from the same instructor in a humorous or a nonhumorous section. (Who knew you could find humor in statistics?) For those students in the humorous section, the instructor incorporated several jokes or cartoons into each lecture, often using humor as a mnemonic device. At the end of the class, the students' final exam scores were analyzed. The students in the humorous section scored, on average, 10 percentage points higher than the students in the nonhumorous section.[1]

So, teachers, take note. If you want to maximize student learning, lighten up. Administrators, if you want to enhance communication with teachers and other staff, lighten up. And that's what this little book is about—lightening up, having a laugh.

Researchers in various fields have repeatedly proven that humor is just plain good for you. Medical researchers, for example, have long known that a hearty laugh can reduce stress, lower your blood pressure, elevate your mood, boost your immune system, improve how your brain functions, and protect your heart. Humor can reduce anxiety and help you cope with the vicissitudes of life. Laughter, the scientists have shown us, decreases stress

---

[1]See Ziv, Avner. "Teaching and Learning With Humor: Experiment and Replication," *Journal of Experimental Education,* Vol. 57, 1988. For a more recent examination of the field, see Rod A. Martin's book, *The Psychology of Humor: An Integrative Approach* (Academic Press, 2007).

hormones and increases infection-fighting antibodies. Besides, it just feels good to laugh.

A half-century ago legendary editor Stanley M. Elam transformed a simple fraternity magazine into the influential education journal that the *Phi Delta Kappan* is today. Since that time readers also have found laughter tucked among the scholarly articles in the cartoons that have traditionally salted the journal's pages. Ninety percent of readers thumb the pages of each issue to read the cartoons first, before they settle into the articles. Okay, unlike Ziv's numbers, that's a made-up statistic. The real figure is probably closer to 99 percent. The *Kappan* is to the world of education journals what *The New Yorker* is to the universe of general magazines.

In this volume, as in previous *Kappan* cartoon collections, the editors have gathered the best of the best from the many cartoons that have appeared in the journal over the years. These cartoons are bound to bring a knowing smile, a wry grin, or a full-out belly laugh. Along with the fun, they may also inspire thoughts about how to incorporate humor into teaching, administration, and parenting. To help you do so, a rotating selection of cartoons is available at **go.solution-tree.com/cartoons** and **pdkintl.org/kappan** for electronic download. We encourage you to visit regularly and download those cartoons for use in meetings to help break the ice, keep spirits high, and motivate you through the serious work of education. —*Donovan Walling*

1. It Takes a Village

Schools and whole districts often are characterized as education villages. The adult inhabitants—from the superintendent or the principal to the guidance counselors, teachers, and parents—are, in theory, focused on rearing and teaching children and young adults of the village. Of course, most schools, even the bright, shiny new ones, also can be like very old villages: prone to arcane traditions and occasionally fraught with bad juju. Village streets were once goat paths, so they wind and twist. And it's common to encounter obstacles—usually the inhabitants themselves, the young, the old, and the in-between. Especially the in-betweens.

"*Ora na azu nwa.*" That's the Nigerian Igbo culture's way of saying, "It takes a village to raise a child." Hillary Rodham Clinton used the phrase as the title of her 1996 book. The media took it from African proverb to American catchphrase faster than a New York minute. Soon it was much parodied, satirized, and sometimes downright maligned. Still, satire aside, there is a kernel of truth in the saying, though as the cartoonists in this chapter often point out, no village is without a resident idiot or two.

Here, then, are cartoons for all who have lived, worked, or perhaps merely visited the village and observed that some residents seem to be one neuron short of a synapse. Have they drunk at the fountain of knowledge or only gargled? Either way, as the youngster whose father was dismayed at his low class standing put it, "Dad, they teach the same thing at both ends." So whether you're high on the totem pole or just watching the villagers dance around it, welcome to the village.

1

"No, Miss Shumway, as a very busy superintendent of schools, I don't have ulcers. I'm a carrier."

"I wonder what kind of super powers he possesses?"

"You've already made up your mind on this, haven't you?"

"I see the board still hasn't found a new superintendent."

"The institutional review has determined that this is the reason your students are falling through the cracks."

"I'm forced to teach to the test. Let's hope you can all look forward to careers as test-takers!"

"As you know, Miss Henson, the school board has had to stretch its resources rather thin. Could I have some of your lunch?"

"Sorry, kids, but this is the newest map we could afford."

"No wonder our education system is in trouble.
Two of the three Rs don't even start with an r."

"If your friends told you to fly into a
windshield, would you do that, too?"

"Don't worry, mom. Our bus driver won't forget."

"Oh ... do you have children?"

"A person changes a lot during adolescence. Since you turned 13, your mother and I have aged 30 years!"

"Someday we're hoping to release him back into the wild."

"Let's have refreshments on parents' night.
These people need nourishment."

"Mom says she'll come to the PTA meeting
if you'll come to her Tupperware party."

"I have to ace this final. My mom already bought a
'My Kid Made the Honor Roll' bumper sticker."

"Today I was visited by nine students and two teachers."

"I would suggest that you get a good education, find a job that pays well, and be happy. I wish I could be more specific."

"I think I need help. I'm hooked on phonics."

2. Teach the Child, Not the Subject

It has always been the mantra of progressive education: "Teach the child, not the subject." It harkens to the theories of well-known progressives, such as John Dewey, Jean Piaget, and Lev Vygotsky, and a whole crop of more recent constructivists. Distilled to its essence, it means reversing the traditional teacher-centered understanding of the learning process and putting students at the center of the process. Well, that's good in theory and sometimes in practice. But, the traditionalist asks, isn't it a bit like putting Curious George in charge of the zoo?

There's an old joke about a mother who wakes up her son: "Time to get up! Time to go to school!"

The son whines, "But, Mom, I don't want to go to school. It's a jungle, and all the kids make fun of me."

To which the mother responds, "I'm sorry, son. You have to go. You're the principal."

Kappan cartoonists often have poked fun at the trials and tribulations of teachers and administrators who are trying their best in trying times—times when "managing" classrooms and corridors looks more like wrangling wild animals. Off to the zoo . . .

"It's not exactly a note from the teacher.
It's more like a joint communiqué from the faculty."

"As a student teacher, the first thing you must learn is how to make your kids behave for you. My own successful disciplinary formula is based on understanding, firmness, determination, and all the bribery I can afford."

"I know you were elected class president,
but that doesn't mean you're in charge..."

"Et tu, Ms. Jones?"

"I brought a jury of my peers."

"Your classroom management techniques work in practice but not in theory. That worries me."

"First, you have to get their attention."

"Due to all the trouble your imaginary friend got you into last year, we transferred him to another class this year."

"I had a *great* day at school.
The principal should be calling any time now. . . ."

"I understand you've achieved
name recognition in the principal's office."

"I thought your lesson plan was very nice . . .
but let's talk about classroom management."

"The teacher said I was trying today. Very trying."

"She told me to clean out my desk, so I assumed I was fired."

"I have this fantasy of being the director of the
nursing home you'll eventually be sent to."

3. Teach the Subject, Not the Child

It's only fair to let the traditionalists have their say. School is about *content*—the three Rs and a few other letters of the alphabet. After all, we've come a long way since schoolteachers were expected to "sweep the floor daily, scrub the floor with soap and water once a week, and start a fire in the stove by 7:00 a.m. so that the classroom will be warm by 8:00," as was the case in 1915. Honestly, it was common for teachers' contracts to contain such provisions.

Over the years, schools have become more complicated, more regimented. Welcome to the six-period day, for example. Our school cartoons in this chapter touch some familiar bases:

- First Period: Art
- Second Period: Math
- Third Period: Science
- Fourth Period: Language Arts
- Fifth Period: History and Geography
- Sixth Period: Research and Study Skills

The only subject missing is computer science, but then, kids learn that in their cradle these days. Take the first-grader whose teacher said, "Billy, spell *cat*." The eager youngster responded, "C- A-T, enter."

Speaking of spelling, there also was the knowing third-grader who advised his younger sibling, "Don't learn to spell *cat*. If you do, the words just keep getting harder."

But whether students handprint their homework on the old ruled paper with the dotted line in the center or type it into a computer, they and their teachers are still subject to all the quirks of the learning process, as the cartoons in this chapter show.

"Yes, some adults paint like that,
but we expect more from children."

"Barry's drawing—his mother is a dentist."

"I don't think you're a bad artist, honey.
Why do you say that?"

"We had some creative differences."

"I paint what I see."

"The amazing thing is, he's never seen a Jackson Pollock!"

"My goal one day is to have my art
hanging on a refrigerator in the Louvre."

"What do you expect? My edition of the math book doesn't have the answers in it like yours does."

"Why can't we put aside petty
partisan bickering and *both* be right?"

"I plan on becoming a mechanic when I grow up.
Would you settle for an estimate?"

"No, Billy, the difference between
10 and 6 is not a rather gray area."

"Of course you have problems! You're a math teacher."

"Aren't there enough problems in the world already?"

Third Period:
Science

"Remember this test, Ms. Hart? 1990.
Multiple choice. You asked which one of these
is not a planet, and I checked Pluto. . . ."

"I'm not sure what Mr. Ziegler has got planned
for class today, but, quite frankly, I'm worried."

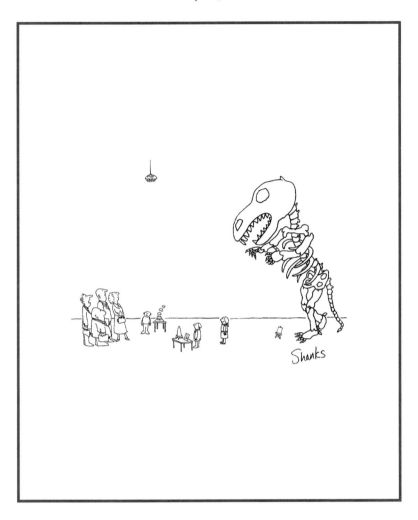

"I believe this one will go down in science fair history."

"Earth science, close up."

"They must really think we're slow readers.
They gave us all summer to read this list,
and I read it on the way down the hall."

"What I like about talking is that
you don't have to worry about spelling."

"Boy, am I in trubbal!"

"Richard, let's have a talk about margins and report lengths."

"My report is called 'The Perils of Plagiarism.'
I copied it off the Internet."

"No, I didn't just copy my report off the Internet. I did it the old-fashioned way. I copied it out of the encyclopedia."

"They're words, Eddie. Assembly required."

"Sorry, Martin—you have to spell the whole word.
You can't just buy a vowel."

"Turns out Joan of Arc wasn't Noah's wife."

"Sure, history's easy for you. You've *lived* it!"

"The Pilgrim kids had corn pudding. We have
pumpkin pie. I guess parents have always tried
to pass vegetables off as dessert."

"I think the Amazon flows into eBay."

"Are you sure Ms. Crawford didn't mean *President* Garfield?"

"You think *your* teacher's old?
Mine teaches history from memory."

"When he said *Klondike*, I thought he meant bars. When he said *Quaker*, I thought he meant oats. When he said *Philadelphia*, I thought he meant cheese. I would've done better if the test had been after lunch."

"They say that history repeats itself—
and, in your case, it might be next semester."

"I don't know how I was supposed to find the English Channel.
I didn't even have the remote control."

"If I go to the library and do my homework,
then it won't really be homework, will it?"

"Just browsing? You can do that without a computer?"

"Do you have anything new by Ernest Hemingway?"

"Sorry—you'll have to find the self-help books on your own."

"An encyclopedia? I don't know.
Let's look up what it is on Wikipedia."

4. A Hunger for Knowledge

Regular *Kappan* readers may remember two previous hunger-related cartoon collections: *My Homework Ate My Dog* and its sequel, *My Homework Ate My Dog Again*. In this take on the hunger theme, our cartoonists look at various aspects, from school lunches to those familiar "hungry for knowledge" breaks from academe: recess and field trips.

Speaking of school lunches, many of us remember the cafeterias of earlier times, when hair-netted lunch ladies of a certain age served up hot meals, and a cute grin could bag you an extra cookie. That recalls a story making the rounds about two little chums in the lunch line at a parochial school. When they came to a pyramid of bright red apples, they noticed a sign: "Take just one . . . God is watching!" Later along the serving line, they spied a mound of cookies. One little fellow elbowed the other and said, "Look! We can take as many cookies as we want. God's watching the apples."

These days, you can buy a prepackaged lunch from a franchise restaurant, snacks from vending machines, and a lunch lady action figure on the Internet. But before you do, check out the cartoons in this chapter.

"The school is serving more nutritious meals,
so I've started to bring my own lunch."

"What's the 'catch of the day'?"

"Too much beanie and not enough weenie."

"Mrs. Smith, there's been a change
in our milk subsidy program."

"They tried adding healthy snacks to the school vending machines, but all that rotting fruit made the candy bars taste bad."

"They never quit, do they?"

"My dad prepared my lunch today."

"I'm much better at computer baseball."

"I guess it's some kind of primitive PlayStation."

"Field trip? Actually, due to budget cuts,
this is now our classroom."

"Our job is to make sure that there is no child left behind."

"When I approved your field trip, Ms. Harris,
I assumed you'd be going along with your class."

5. Making the Grade

The cartoons in this chapter highlight the travails of students making it through school, with special attention to report cards (listen for the groan), homework (louder groan), and graduation (woohoo!).

Readers of education history—or those who have simply lived long enough—will be quick to note that there's not a lot of difference between today's report cards and those that students carried home a century ago. It's been said that if Thomas Edison came back from the grave, he wouldn't recognize anything except the report card—and his report cards were no great shakes. Young Edison's teachers considered him "addled," and so his formal education was cut short, almost before it had begun. Yet little Thomas became a voracious reader, set up his first laboratory at age ten, and at twelve established a lab in an empty freight car on the Grand Trunk Railway. He also began printing a weekly newspaper, the *Grand Trunk Herald.*

This topic brings to mind a story about a little girl who asked, "Daddy, can you write in the dark?"

Her father replied, "Sure, I guess so. What do I need to write?"

"Oh," said the girl, "just your name when you sign my report card."

Then there were the parents who were disappointed in their son's report card. "Our only consolation," lamented his mother, "is that we know he didn't cheat."

A good laugh has always eased the pain of parents and teachers alike. So on to the cartoons!

"On the right is your painting of 'A Snowman in a Blizzard,'
and on the left is your book report written in invisible ink.
I'm beginning to see a pattern here."

"I'm good under pressure. I can get all my homework done during the commercials."

"The subject was inexplicable, so I didn't try to explick it."

"Just because you've eaten a lot of homework
doesn't mean you have a book in you."

"Boy! If we learn from our mistakes,
today should have made me pretty smart."

"My brother ate my homework."

"I couldn't do my homework
because I was working on my blog."

"It turns out my dog didn't eat last month's homework.
I found it when my mom made me clean my room."

"I, too, didn't think that cats ate homework."

"I can't come to school today because I have
a barking cough. Wanna hear it?"

"If you think it will help, yeah, let's hear your spin."

"Dad didn't sign my report card,
but as you can see, I did show it to him."

"Don't blame me. You're the one who
urged me to think outside the box."

"It seems his hunger for knowledge went on a diet."

"I tell my dad our report cards are now being issued online,
and he won't admit he can't access them."

"Ignorance *isn't* bliss."

"Please, Mother, not yet!"

Payback comes for the class clown

6. Plugged In

Remember that Sixties slogan: "Turn on, tune in, drop out"? Decades later, it has new meaning when applied to today's technologically plugged-in kids.

Today's Facebooked, YouTubed, Twittered, video-gamed, and texted generation plugs in whatever device is handy—a computer, a GameCube, a music player, a cell phone—turns it on, tunes it in, and drops out of the mundane world and into a universe that even Alice in Wonderland would find hard to imagine.

Are you or your students *too* plugged in? Consider these indicators: Do all your friends have @ signs in their names? Does your dog have its own homepage? Do you believe that you can safely send text messages while driving? Think about it.

The cartoons in this chapter are for those comfortable with new technology as well as those who, at some point, have plugged the power strip cord into the power strip itself and wondered why the computer wouldn't turn on.

"If your cell phone has 500 minutes,
and you use one of them during this math class,
how long will you be in detention?"

"Okay, which one of you has the cell phone ringtone
that sounds like a class bell?"

"No homework for the first one
who can show me how to use my new phone."

"Then I said to Ms. Rand, 'Do you mind? I'm on the phone.'"

"Can I call you back? This isn't a good time."

"If you have a question, Robert,
just come up here to my desk."

"If I have to keep both hands on the wheel,
how will I check my text messages?"

"Yes, I heard the sea. But does it take photos?"

"It was embarrassing. While I was taking away
their cell phones, my cell phone rang."

"I'm not going to school today. I think I caught a cold from an open window on my computer."

"It's the technical support number . . .
kind of a homework hotline for grown-ups."

"The computer makes it easier for me to do all the things
I never needed to do before I got a computer."

"It's not easy getting all your homework done
between dinnertime and prime time."

"They put me in the slow class at school
because I have dial-up Internet service."

"For the last time, this is called
'current events,' not 'Headline News.'"

"I don't get it! They make us learn reading, writing,
and arithmetic to prepare us for a world of videotapes,
computer terminals, and calculators!"

"I'm taking an innovative approach
to teaching this semester. I'm using books!"

"When do we learn to blog?"

"Does this pen come in another font?"

"They're very easy to operate.
The pointy end is enter, and the pink end is delete."

"I discovered you can change the font size
of this pencil just by sharpening it."

"My teacher says the Internet encyclopedia may be
fictitious and inaccurate. The Internet encyclopedia
says my teacher may be technophobic and old-fashioned."

7. The Teachers' Lounge

Ah, the teachers' lounge—that haven, that refuge from the maddening crowd. Look closely. You can tell a veteran teacher from a newcomer; the veteran always checks the seat of the chair before sitting down. The veteran teacher is the one who volunteers for hall duty on days when faculty meetings are scheduled, but also the one who instinctively—and without conscious awareness—picks up litter while walking down the hallway.

A true teacher knows that students can teach them many things, such as how much patience the teacher has. Sometimes it's the questions students come up with that send the caffeine-deprived teacher scurrying for the teachers' lounge the moment the dismissal bell rings. Questions such as:

"If you're in a spaceship going the speed of light, what happens when you turn on the headlights?"

"What do you plant to grow seedless grapes?"

"Why doesn't glue stick to the inside of the glue bottle?"

As might be expected in our electronic age, a number of virtual teachers' lounges have cropped up on the Internet. They provide "places" in the ether where teachers can share ideas, find answers, and blog about issues. Many, in fact, are sponsored by local school districts. But all of them have one glaring deficiency in common: you can't get coffee in a virtual teachers' lounge.

Fortunately, you can find a laugh or two to lighten the load. And that, of course, is the purpose of the cartoons in this chapter.

"Ms. Henson, you're going in for Ms. Bleckmore."

"Well, if they asked me to come up with a substitute for a teacher, another teacher would be the last thing on my list."

"Hard morning, Patricia?"

"The kids don't listen, so I have to repeat myself.
I'm always repeating myself. You know, always saying
the same thing more than once. I say it once,
and they make me say it again. . . . "

"I love it. Just shake it up, and it's a snow day."

"No, I don't get overtime for keeping you after school."

"Do you realize that they pay our teacher
to come to school every day and we do it for free?"

"You're a teacher. You should know better
than to grade papers on a curve."

"I realize you're overworked,
and that's why you're so valuable."

"So, other than that, how was your first day as a teacher?"

"I see a lot of men coming into your life. Unfortunately,
they're all 9-year-olds and don't want to do their homework."

"So, Ms. Burton, how long have you been
teaching grade school?"

About the Artists

George Abbott

A retired postal worker, George Abbott has been cartooning for several years. His wife, Marianne, helps prepare cartoons for mailing and offers advice and encouragement. Abbott's first big sale was to the *National Enquirer*; since then, his cartoons have appeared in most major magazines and in many trade journals, as well as in several collections. "I do a few, I sell a few," he says. Since retirement, he divides his time between cartooning and model railroading.

Charles Almon

Charles Almon works full time as an artist, writer, and cartoonist in historic Brooklyn Heights, New York. He hopes the Obama administration is serious about tackling the problems that have caused our once-enviable education system to take a backseat to other industrialized countries. A little humor couldn't hurt.

Aaron Bacall

Aaron Bacall has graduate degrees in organic chemistry and in educational administration and supervision from New York University. He has been a pharmaceutical research chemist, college departmental coordinator, college instructor, and cartoonist. His work has appeared in most national publications and in several cartoon collections. His work has been used for advertising, greeting cards, wall calendars, and several corporate promotional books. Three of his cartoons are featured in the permanent collection at the Harvard Business School's Baker Library. He continues to create and sell his cartoons. Aaron can be reached at abacall@msn.com.

Edouard Blais

Edouard Blais was born and raised in St. Paul, Minnesota. He graduated from St. Cloud State University with a degree in art education. He also did post-graduate work at the University of Minnesota and the Minneapolis Institute of Arts. Edouard taught art for thirty-two years at the elementary and middle school levels in Biwabik and Robbinsdale, Minnesota. He has been cartooning for over twenty-five years, and his work has been published in magazines, newspapers, and trade journals across the United States and Canada.

Art Bouthillier

Art Bouthillier has been a freelance cartoonist for over twenty years. He lives with his wife and daughter on idyllic Whidbey Island in Washington state. Art owes his inspiration to greats such as Don Martin, Sergio Aragones, Ozzy Osbourne, and Abe Vigoda.

Martin J. Bucella

Marty Bucella has been a full-time, freelance cartoonist/humorous illustrator since 1977. His sales to magazines, newspapers, greeting card companies, book publishers, and the web have topped the 300,000 mark. To see more of Marty's work, visit his website at www.martybucella.com.

Ford Button

Jazz guitarist, history buff, father of five, grandfather of three, art teacher, and cartoonist for over thirty years, Ford Button was all of these and more. His experience as an educator provided the inspiration for his work. Ford's cartoons have appeared in *Good Housekeeping,* the *National Enquirer, Better Homes and Gardens, Family Circle,* and in many trade, technical, and fraternal magazines. Though Ford left us in 1995, his inspiration will live on—as he said, "The nice thing about humor is that you don't have to get a prescription for it!"

Martha Campbell

Martha Campbell is a graduate of the School of Fine Arts, Washington University, St. Louis, and a former writer and designer for Hallmark Cards. She has been a freelance cartoonist and illustrator since leaving Hallmark. She lives in Harrison, Arkansas.

Dave Carpenter

Dave Carpenter has been a full-time cartoonist since 1981. Besides the *Phi Delta Kappan,* his cartoons have appeared in such publications as *Harvard Business Review, Reader's Digest, The Wall Street Journal, Woman's World, First for Women, The Saturday Evening Post, Good Housekeeping, The National Law Journal,* and a number of other publications, including the *Chicken Soup for the Soul* books. He can be contacted at davecarp@ncn.net.

Frank Cotham

Frank Cotham has had cartoons published by a number of magazines, including *The New Yorker, The Wall Street Journal, Barron's,* and *The Saturday Evening Post.* He held a number of jobs before becoming a cartoonist, but he considers cartooning "the most satisfying by far."

James Estes

A full-time cartoonist for more than thirty-five years, James Estes numbers among his clients *Woman's World, The Wall Street Journal, Ebony, Highlights for Children,* and *The Saturday Evening Post,* along with the *Phi Delta Kappan.* He is married to his wife, Martha, and has three children: Robert, a West Point graduate; Kelley, a special education coordinator; and Paige, an elementary school music teacher. James and Martha have five grandchildren.

Randy Glasbergen

Randy Glasbergen's cartoons are seen all over the world in newspapers, magazines, greeting cards, books, advertising, and even taxi cabs. He creates "The Better Half" for King Features and "Thin Lines" for Creators Syndicate. You can find more of Randy's cartoons at www.glasbergen.com.

Patrick Hardin

Patrick Hardin is a freelance cartoonist and illustrator whose work appears internationally in a variety of books and publications. He can be contacted at phardin357@aol.com.

Jonny Hawkins

Jonny Hawkins has been professionally drawing cartoons for over twenty years, with sales to over four hundred publications. He has three block calendars ("Medical Cartoon-A-Day," "Fishing Cartoon-A-Day," and "Car 'Toons Laugh-A-Day"), as well as several books on the market. A dog humor and a cat humor collection will be published in 2009. He lives in Sherwood, Michigan with his wife, Carissa, and their three young children.

Nick Hobart

Nick Hobart was born in London and attended Dulwich College. After working in a bank and teaching, he and his family immigrated to Canada. It was there that he began cartooning and became a regular contributor to *Punch, Spectator,* and the *Canadian Review,* edited by a young Graydon Carter. He lives on Florida's Suncoast, where he enjoys bicycling and growing roses.

Norman Jung

For as long as he can remember, Norman Jung always wanted to be a cartoonist. He made his first cartoon sale to *Home Life* magazine while serving in the Air Force. After he was discharged, he studied commercial art and earned his BA at San Jose State University, and then worked as an advertising artist for three newspapers. He has been a freelance cartoonist for over twenty years.

Kyle Kaser

Kyle Kaser was born in Oregon in 1930. He attended the Portland Art Museum School and graduated from Portland State University. After teaching high school art for seven years, he began a new career in industrial and school safety. He has a longtime interest in cartooning and his work has appeared in *Principal* and *Phi Delta Kappan* magazines. Since retirement, he continues cartooning, painting, and writing.

Scott Arthur Masear

Scott Arthur Masear has sold his work to many publications over twenty years of cartooning. The *Phi Delta Kappan* is one of his favorite magazines to draw for—and it was also one of the first markets that supported him in the early days.

Stephanie Piro

Stephanie Piro is an award-winning cartoonist, illustrator, and designer. She is one of King Features' team of women cartoonists, "Six Chix" (she is the "Saturday Chick"). She also does the daily comic, "Fair Game," that appears on her website www.stephaniepiro.com, and in magazines, books, calendars, and cards. Check out the "Chix" blog at www.thesixchix.com and contact her at stephaniepiro@gmail.com.

Robert Schochet

Robert Schochet of Highland Mills, New York, has been creating cartoons for twenty-five years, and for the most part, enjoying every minute of it. Working as a freelance cartoonist, he has published award-winning cartoons in such major magazines and newspapers as *Good Housekeeping, Cosmopolitan, Playboy,* the *National Enquirer, Better Homes and Gardens,* and *The Wall Street Journal.*

H. L. Schwadron

Based in Ann Arbor, Michigan, Harley Schwadron has been a freelance cartoonist for many years, working for *Barron's, The Wall Street Journal,* and the *Harvard Business Review,* in addition to the *Phi Delta Kappan.* He worked as a newspaper reporter and college news bureau and alumni magazine editor before becoming a full-time cartoonist. Currently, he also does a daily business panel, "9 to 5," syndicated by Chicago Tribune Media Services, and works as an op-ed cartoonist for many newspapers. He can be contacted at schwaboo@comcast.net.

Al Sens

Al Sens was born in Vancouver and attended the Vancouver School of Art. He has published cartoons in both American and Canadian magazines. He also produced, directed, and animated short cartoons and commercials (under the name Al Sens Animation Ltd.) for television in the United States, Canada, and numerous European countries. Additionally, Al taught animation at the University of British Columbia in Vancouver. Now semiretired, he continues to draw cartoons.

John R. Shanks

John Shanks lives in a suburb of Atlanta with his wife, Deb. He is a senior research specialist in the biochemistry department at Emory University. His cartoons have appeared in the *Phi Delta Kappan, The Saturday Evening Post,* the *Harvard Business Review,* and other publications. His two sons live nearby with their families. His four grandchildren take turns distracting him while the others loot his art supplies.

Mike Shapiro

Mike Shapiro's cartoons have appeared in many publications, including *The Wall Street Journal, Barron's,* the *Harvard Business Review, USA Today,* and *Reader's Digest.* His work has also been published in countless books and humor collections. A contributor to many legal, medical, and business journals, Mike has also done work for animation studios and advertising agencies. You can see more of his work at www.mikeshapirocartoons.com.

Mike Twohy

Mike Twohy is the creator of the syndicated daily panel "That's Life" and a regular contributor to *The New Yorker.* He lives in Berkeley, California.

Bob Vojtko

It's all cartoons all the time, as Bob Vojtko makes a living poking fun at the human condition. Bob's material stems from his family, friends, and interactions with people in the grocery business, where he has worked for over thirty years. You'll find Vojtko cartoons in newspapers, newsletters, magazines, books, and on the Internet. He lives in Strongsville, Ohio, with his wife, Susan, and their Boston terrier, Massie.

Alejandro Yegros

As well as being a cartoonist, Alejandro Yegros is a high school Spanish teacher in Weston, Massachusetts. Many of the situations (and sometimes, caricatures) in his cartoons come from his classroom experiences. His work also appears in the *Bulletin of the Atomic Scientists.*

Solution Tree | Press

a division of

Solution Tree

Solution Tree's mission is to advance the work of our authors. By working with the best researchers and educators worldwide, we strive to be the premier provider of innovative publishing, in-demand events, and inspired professional development designed to transform education to ensure that all students learn.

The Professional
Association in
Education

Phi Delta Kappa International (PDK) is the premier professional association for educators that includes teachers, principals, superintendents, and higher education faculty and administrators. PDK's mission is to promote high-quality education as essential to the development and maintenance of a democratic way of life. That mission is accomplished through the tenets of leadership, research, and service.